MW01611662

Live
Again

John Stevenson

2009

live again

Red Moon Press
PO Box 2461
Winchester VA
22604-1661 USA
www.redmoonpress.com

First Printing

pretty sure my red is your red

So writes John Stevenson in this, his highly anticipated third full-length volume. If I read this poem correctly, the poet is expecting or hoping that the you in the poem sees the world pretty much as he does. Though he may be addressing a particular individual, it is easy to put myself in her place and affirm, yes, your red is my red. Yes, I feel myself in the presence of a kindred spirit. My expectation is that you will feel this kinship too.

Stevenson writes about life as we live it. In his hands, quotidian moments become poetry. When he invites us to share those "certain moments [he'd] be glad to live again," we are happy to accommodate him.

What distinguishes John Stevenson is his humanity: his willingness to share the unvarnished essence of himself, revealing a deliciously wry sense of humor as well as deep empathy and sympathy for others. He writes:

> reversible jacket
> the side
> I always show

but in this book he dares to show us the other side. That the poems are personal and intimate makes them all the more universal in appeal.

The landscape Stevenson paints can more accurately be described as interiorscape, i.e., the emotional colors of life, with all its subtle and not-so-subtle shadings. Leave it to this accomplished poet to describe it thus:

demolition site
the colors
of closet walls

Stevenson is master of "tell[ing] the whole story in a single breath," and he clearly understands "the way all stories are connected." Sometimes a kigo sets the tone of a poem. Often, though, the poem telegraphs the mood of a particular season without naming it overtly. Stevenson's kigo-less poems, whether you call them haiku or senryu, demonstrate a feeling for the deep connection between Nature and human nature.

the tide
arranging rocks and sand
just as I would

Never one for flourish or embellishment, Stevenson's mature voice is even more spare than it has been in the past. On one level, what you see is what you get. But this being haiku, what you see is never *all* you get. Whether talking about a curled leaf in the chamber of a toy six-shooter, clouds the size of his hometown, or the recognition that "We only behaved according to our natures," Stevenson's imagery is vivid, yet open enough to allow the reader to bring his or her own associations to this moment keenly perceived by the poet.

It is not only Stevenson's voice that is unique, but the ordering and presentation of poems is intriguing as well. Haiku and senryu are interspersed with tanka and haibun; a one-word haiku appears alongside an Einbond Award-winning renku (written in collaboration with Merrill Ann

Gonzales). This creates an exciting element of chance that is not as apparent in Stevenson's earlier collections. At the same time, poems (of whatever length) are so skillfully linked that the reader is drawn deeper and deeper into the "story."

There is an exuberance in this book that is best expressed by Stevenson himself: "soft earth / I might risk / a cartwheel." Perhaps it was at a low point that Stevenson penned:

> midnight sun
> I know for a fact
> the bottle's half empty

However, by the time you come to the end of this outstanding collection by one of the foremost haiku poets of our time, I expect you will know for an absolute fact that the bottle's half full.

Carolyn Hall
San Francisco CA
2009

Live Again

the snow
falls slowly
into place
certain moments I'd be
glad to live again

Live

long night—
breathing until breathing
is just breathing

dawn
before there is any
tune in my head

warming the words
in my mouth—
in winter
one's timing
is everything

almost spring
she tells the whole story
in a single breath

a small favor
repaid
in zucchini

summer ending
press one
to confirm

back to work
after my vacation
on another planet
where I didn't
weigh so much

great clouds
each one the size of
my hometown

A child's
wide eyes
stare at me.
If I could
I'd have a look too.

toy six-shooter
a curled leaf
in the chamber

we're here
we might as well build
a sand castle

I can't
imagine
being born
my mother
so young

soft earth
I might risk
a cartwheel

midnight sun
I know for a fact
the bottle's half empty

fireflies
beyond
the sarcasm

my hands at rest
in dishwater . . .
first hummingbird

rock
hardening
time

rehearsing my words
until I arrive
saying something else

uncertain
which way
to face the scarecrow

he practices safe sex as much as the next guy

again his account
of the airbag inflating
inflating

here
for now
first snow

unable to find the middle of the night

after midnight
getting some of my thoughts
into the lifeboats

UNKNOWN

I take comfort in the fruit of my efforts and those of others, known and unknown, aware that I live in greater comfort than many a king of antiquity.

I am thinking particularly of how it feels curling up with a good book on a winter night, the house warm, a cup of cocoa steaming on the night stand, reading something entertaining and not too challenging. There are so many possibilities. The feeling coming over me is a slightly reluctant but grateful surrender to a full night's sleep.

Sometime during the night, however, I wake and realize I really have been hearing tiny creatures: mice, voles, something scurrying back and forth inside the walls. Extracting tiny claws from my dreams, I remind myself they can't harm me, try to ignore them and go back to sleep. But my imagination has already become engaged and strives, despite my wishes, to a get a sense of where they are, what they are, how many there are . . .

> who tripped
> the mousetrap
> remains a mystery

city moon
generations
of renters

one of your sighs
has stayed with me
forty years, so far

cold night
the dashboard lights
of another car

sparrows sift through
the shopping carts
autumn dusk

while you explain
(too earnestly, it seems to me)
why you're late again
strangers are rushing
to strange places

grown wild
the spot where I buried
the last of my pets

nothing matters how green it gets

summer dusk wine talk of God

pretty sure my red is your red

I sleep with her
or she sleeps with me
autumn equinox

Colonel Mustard
in the library . . .
winter night

low tide —
stones that have dried
among those that haven't

will they get me through
another winter
my furnace, my car
my love
my country

this Halloween,
children born since
9/11

We only behaved
according to our natures,
you and I.
What does the sun know
about shadows?

it feels okay
to have an empty head
sunny afternoon

the width of a leaf between us and autumn

the tide
arranging rocks and sand
just as I would

mid winter
hoping
it's nothing

my doctor
takes off his glasses . . .
cold for May

I put myself
in the shoes
of a dying friend.
He'd moved on by then
in his bare feet . . .

rain washes the street
I've already said
goodnight

jury room —
mutiple errors
in a discarded crossword

words . . .
just one of the things
that we misused

dinner for one
a view
of the ocean

Oscar night
adjusting the cuffs
of my pajamas

class reunion
everybody loved
my wife

a big diamond . . .
just imagine
the pressure

I've learned from you
that words
mean other words

moonlight
tell me what you haven't
told anyone

CITY ON THE HILL
a nijuin renku

John Stevenson / Merrill Ann Gonzales

Opening Section:

city on the hill
offering up
an aura of green

prize peonies
grow in your garden

the language
of the honey bee
in wide use

Bach's Little Fugue
fills the room

Back Section:

crescent moon
at the tip
of a mitten

under Orion I long
for an embracing warmth

Juliet awakens,
as she was promised,
in a tomb

gypsum chandeliers
dazzle in the cave

tandori chicken
arrives at the table
with a sizzle

the feathers must be tied
in just the right way

Second Back Section:

we wander
pathless heavens
in our hot air balloon

fewer this year
at the class reunion

along the boardwalk
the words and looks
of those in love

brushing fallen leaves
from your hair

bright moon
turns the shack
to gold

"I'm supposed to be
Rumplestiltskin!"

Closing Section:

the day
draws near
for the birth

bluffing
with a pair of deuces

morning shadows
strawberry blossoms
for us to find

the beachcomber's
widening smile . . .

❀ ❀ ❀ ❀ ❀

after a journey
of a thousand miles
tv with you

a light touch
the harvest
half-moon

core

summer dawn
an arm raised
for deodorant

long day
a chameleon's
tongue

so much
of what I do
involves my body

unstacking
the teacups
I get to keep

everywhere this week
I remember you said
get lost

someone must be first
to turn away —
moon viewing

checkout line
my dad
could talk to anyone

the unknown man
who stared down the tanks —
we love him
and also the one
who pulled him aside

the way all stories
are connected—
her tremor
reaches me
through the table

humming
humming bird
humming

spring morning
the hand of a student who
may know the answer

thought I was going somewhere March wind

false start
of springtime
I feel it coming
another round
of hating everything

winter drags on more of me than ever

used book store
the creaking stairway
to poetry

my old wallet
in the top drawer
winter darkness

yearbook inscription:
never forget . . .
something illegible

after the play
my grown son tells me
I was good

all grown up
and buying myself
a nightlight

liking the same music
we hope the rest
will be easy

writers' conference —
from a toilet stall I hear
someone quoting me

Christmas evening
the snow
hasn't stuck

winter
the interval
between park benches

cookie crumbs
between Christmas
and the new year

groundhog day—
it doesn't matter
what I see

Again

winter morning where we left off yesterday

a penny for my thoughts?
. . . the fireflies
of last summer

cold moon—
a moment of hesitation
years ago

rehab food
no taste
but the aftertaste
(with Seneca Kennedy)

reversible jacket
the side
I always show

last snow, in the woods,
like the underlining
of an obscure passage

thirty years
on the job
I've become
something of an expert
on what's unimportant

when we met
what we had
in common
was the same kind of
wood burning stove

poor singing voices
nevertheless
they have built a nest

HOW ENVY WORKS

Yu Chang wrote:

> warm kitchen
> the rise and fall
> of friends' laughter

I've often wished I'd written it, or at least that I'd been present at its inspiration. The scene has always seemed to me so full of the goodness of life.

Recently I heard Yu talking about how this poem came to him and realized that I actually had been present . . . four years ago . . . already one of the friends.

winter night
I lie in bed
and imagine it

Memorial Day
some losses
are recent

demolition site
the colors
of closet walls

one of the places
we used to live
violets

gingerbread men
in plastic wrap —
the long night

seated between us
the imaginary
middle passenger

evening calm . . .
the fisherman's
smoke rings

embarrassed
by the lavish praise
I imagine getting

daisy
not waiting
to be asked

end of summer —
shopping for something
less comfortable

a sort of afterlife
coming home
from work

bringing in
some of the cold
when we enter
taking some of the warmth
when we depart

merry-go-round
I think that may be
where I left the map

late night—
the waitress repeats
the list of pies

Some of these poems first appeared (occasionally in slightly different form) in the following publications: *Acorn, ant 5, Brussels Sprout, Geppo, Hermitage, Frogpond, Kusa-makura Contest, Mainichi Daily News, Mariposa, Modern Haiku, Pilgrimage, Raw Nervz, Red Lights, Ribbons, Roadrunner, Rusty Paper Clip (HNA Anthology), Shamrock Haiku Journal, Simply Haiku, The Heron's Nest, Tanka Society of America Newsletter, Tundra, Upstate Dim Sum*

Thanks to my writing partners for permission to reproduce their work here (and for the pleasure of working with them).

*Yu Chang
Merrill Ann Gonzales
Seneca Kennedy*

For their editorial assistance, my thanks to Yu Chang, Tom Clausen, Carolyn Hall, Jim Kacian, and Hilary Tann.

My thanks to Shiki Prize winner Cor van den Heuvel for the inspiration he has provided me and for all he has done and continues to do on behalf of English-language haiku.